Christmas

TODDLER COLORING BOOK

· Little-One Coloring Books ·

Copyright: Published in the United States by Little-One Coloring Books
Published December 2017

ISBN-10: 1981444157
ISBN-13: 978-1981444151

Hello !
My name is

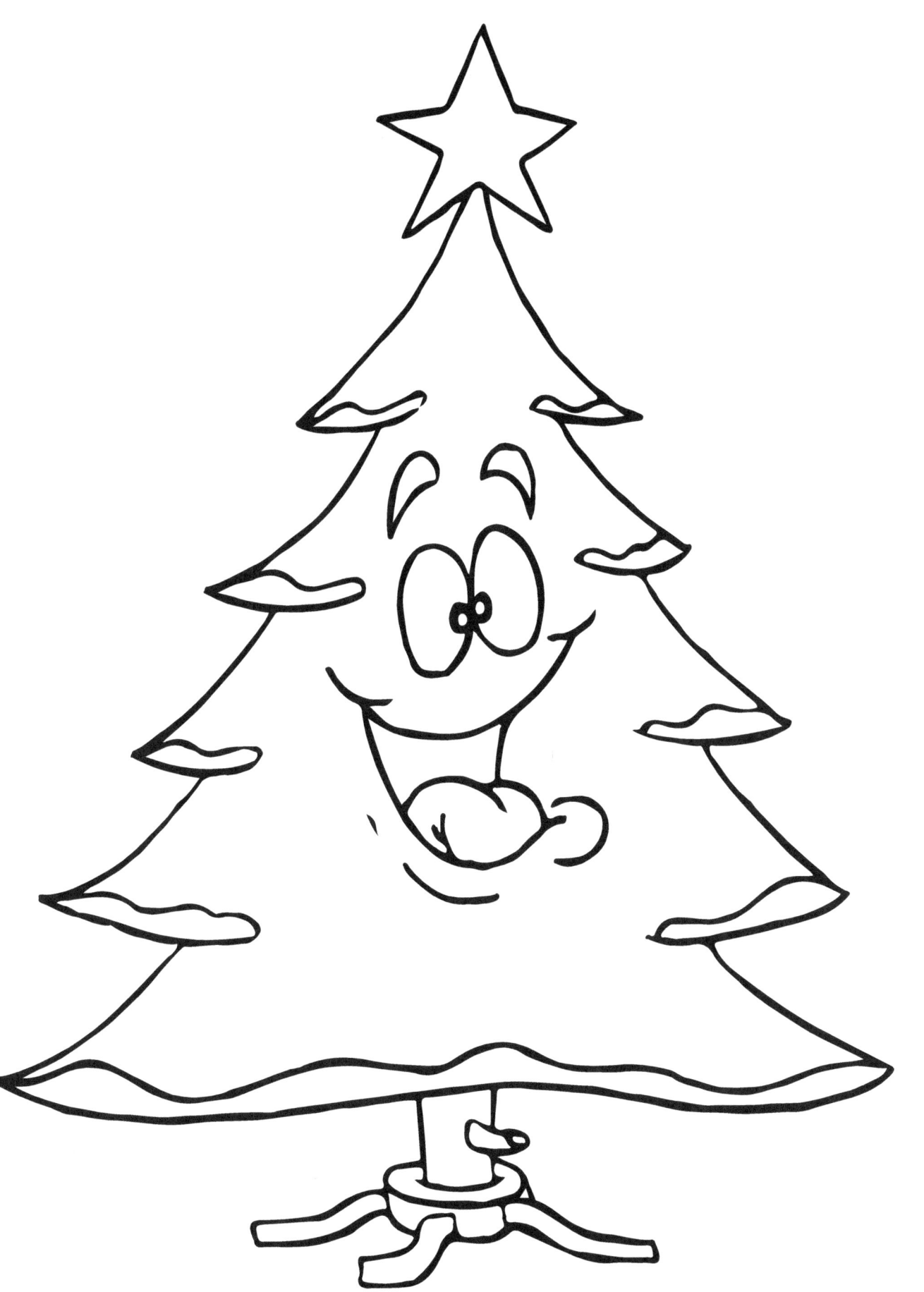

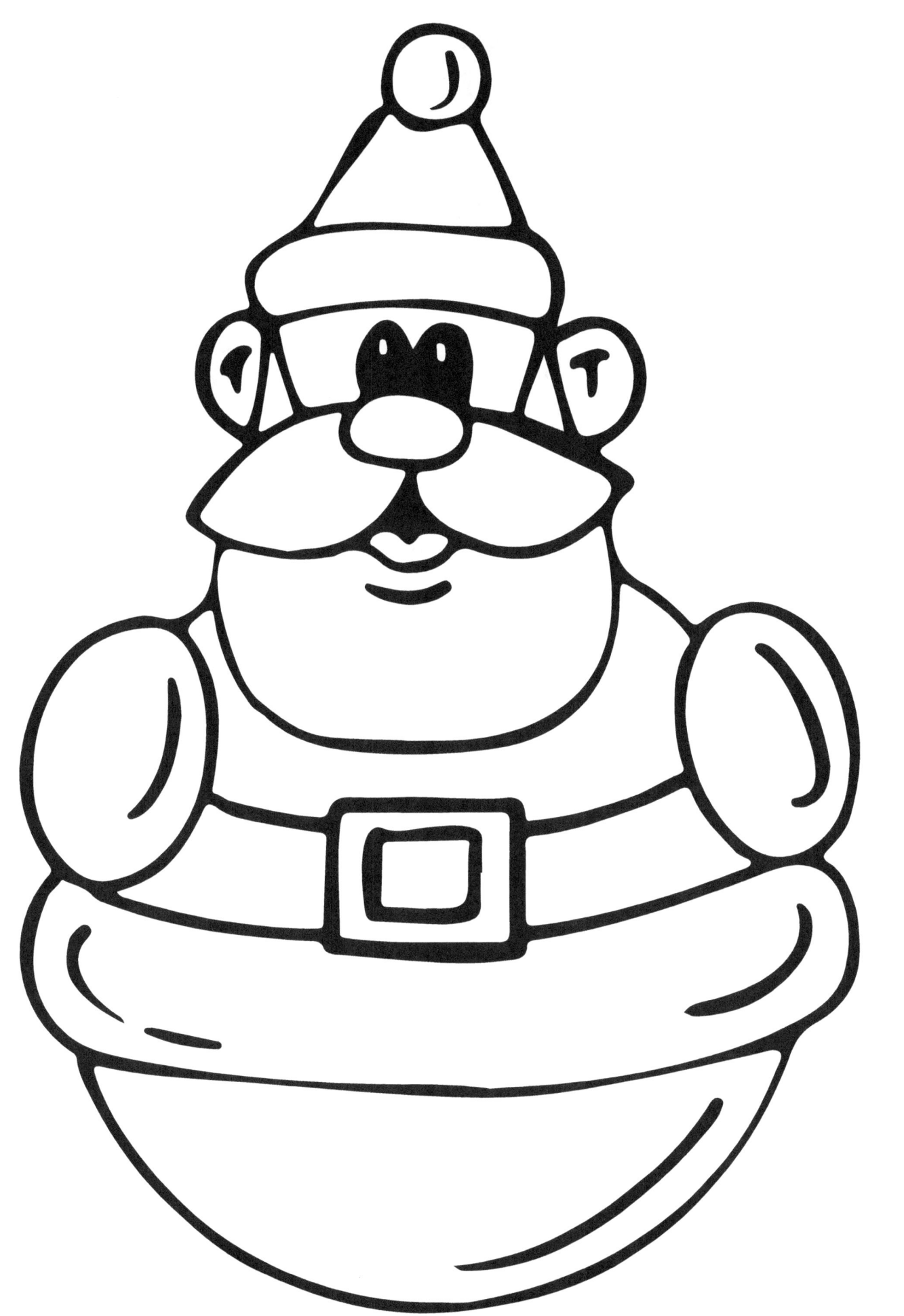

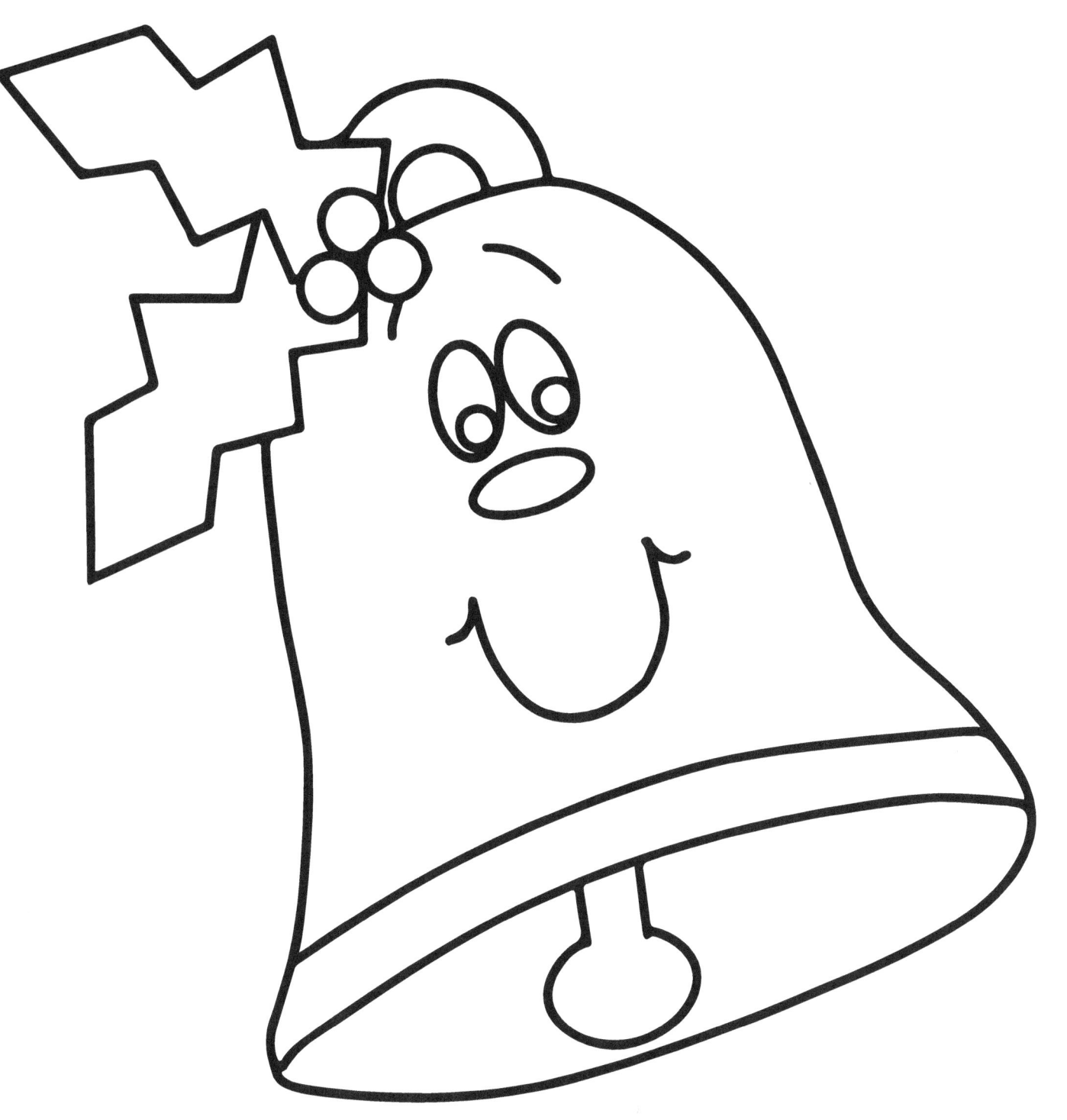

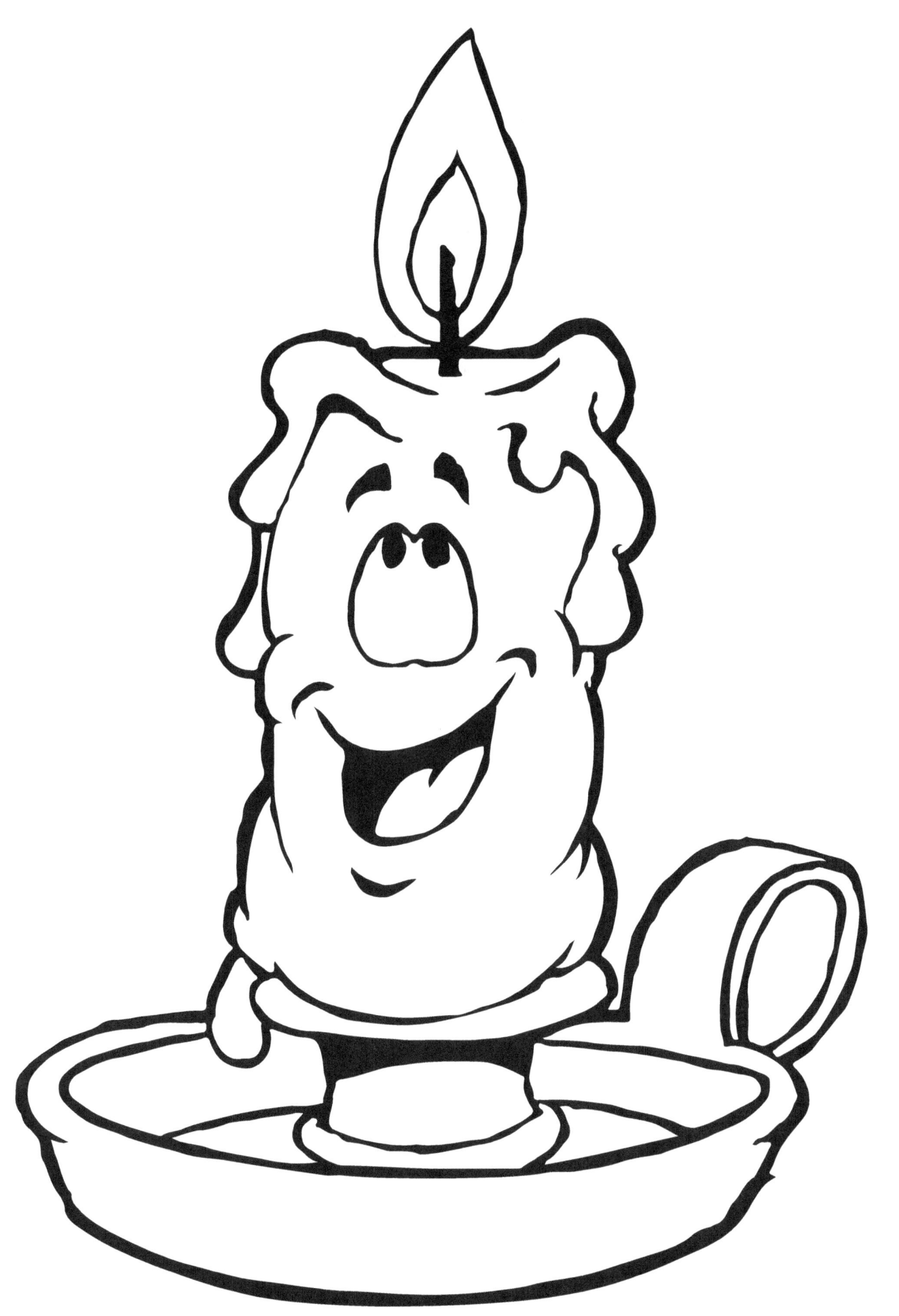

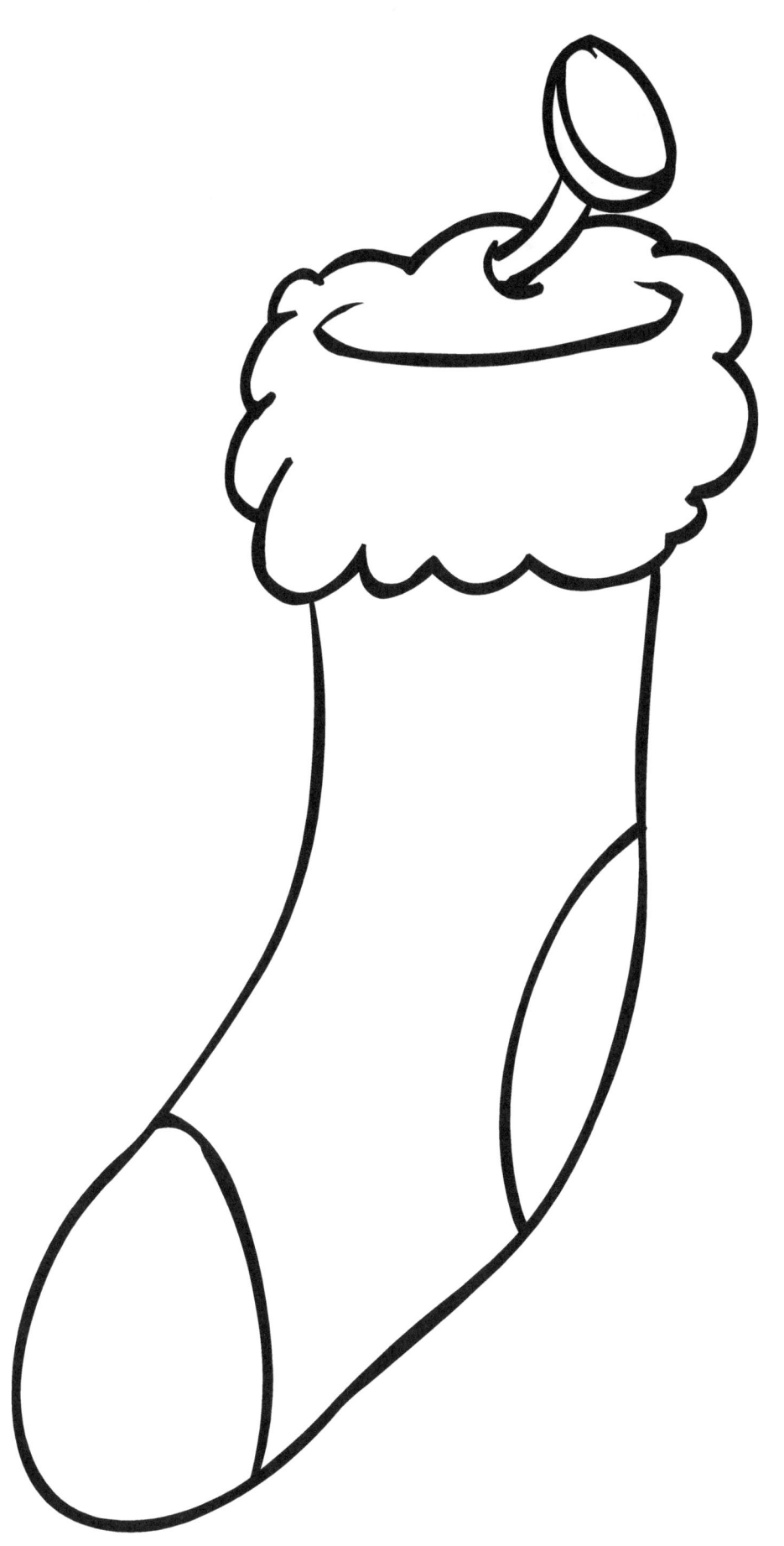

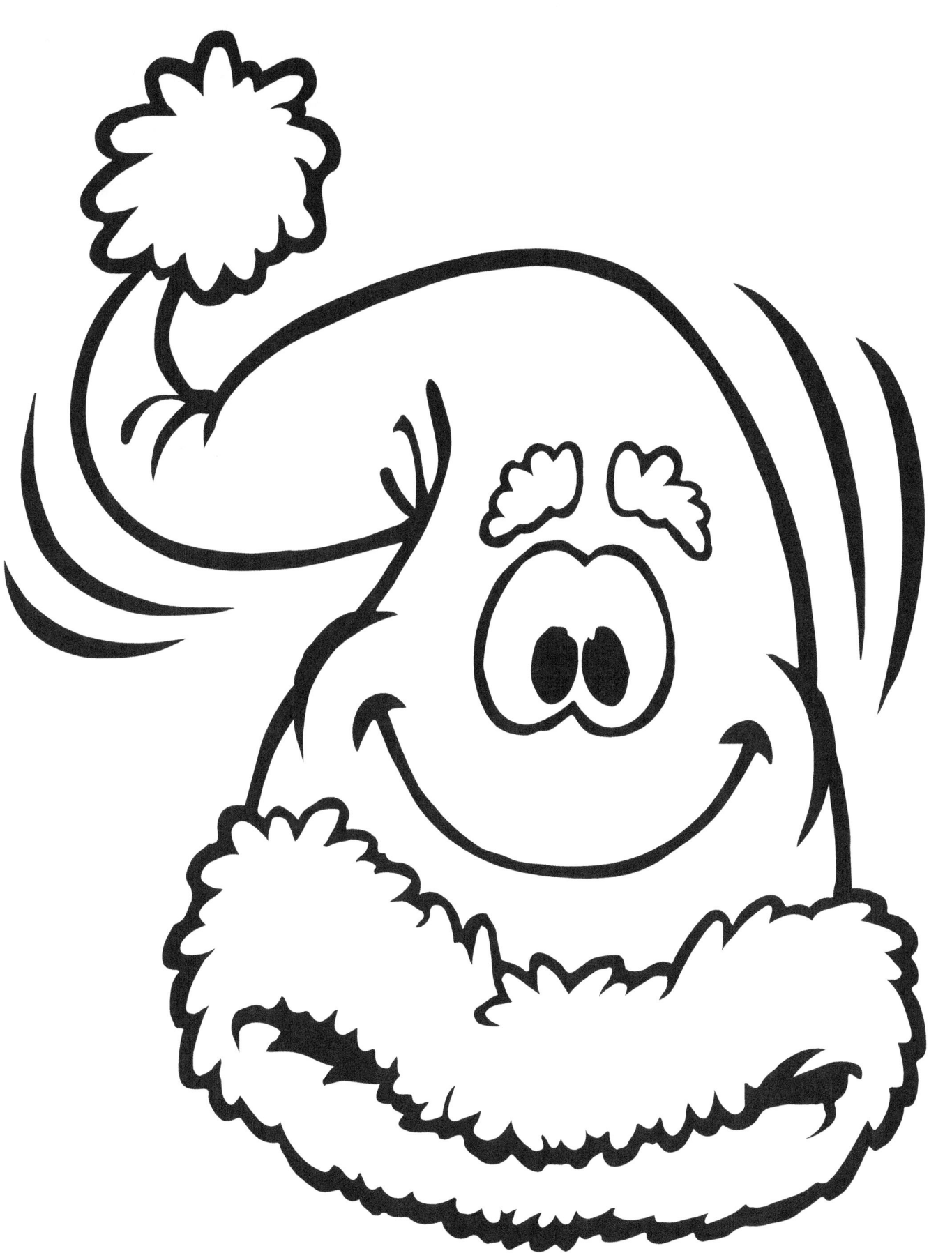

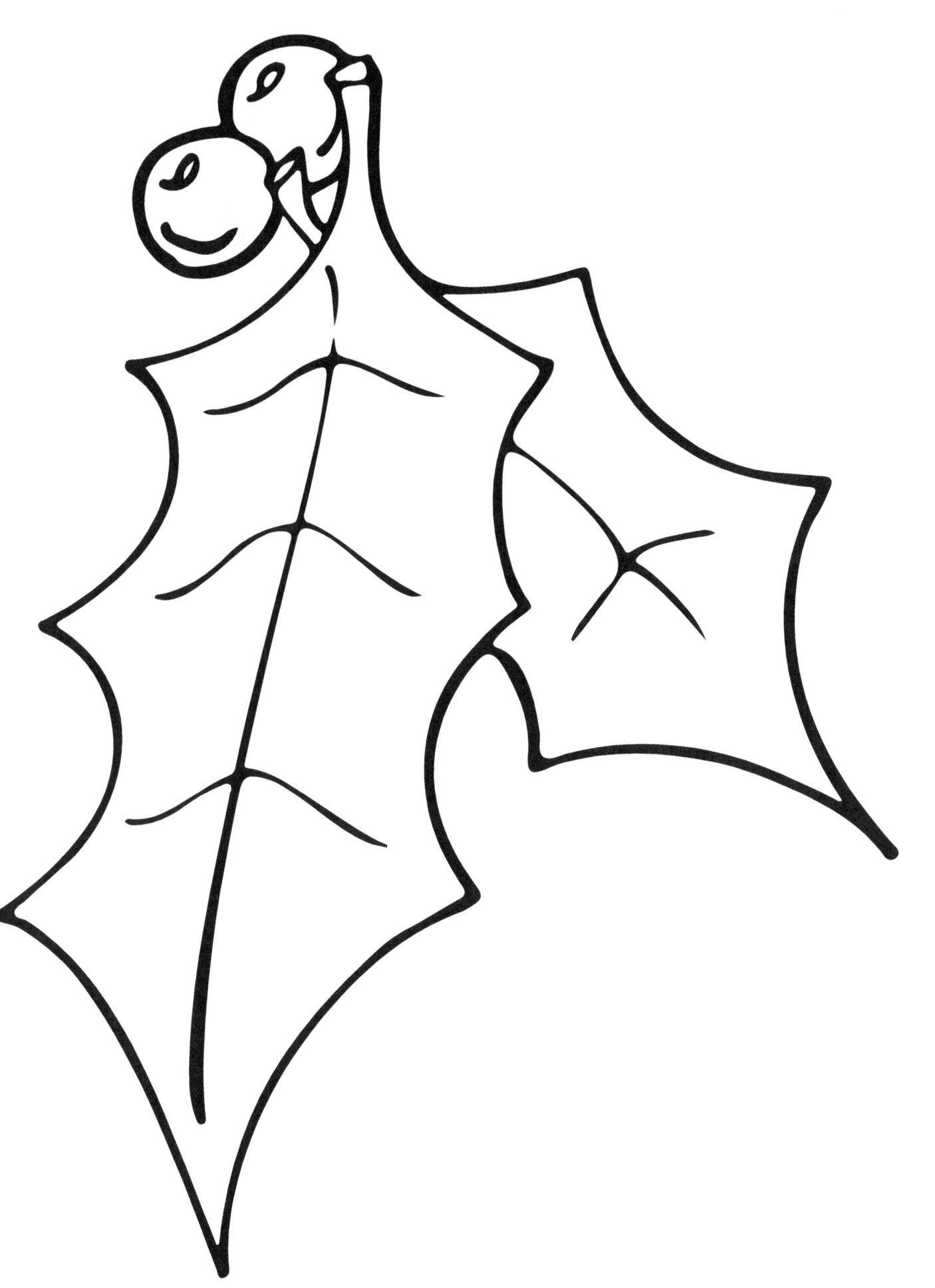

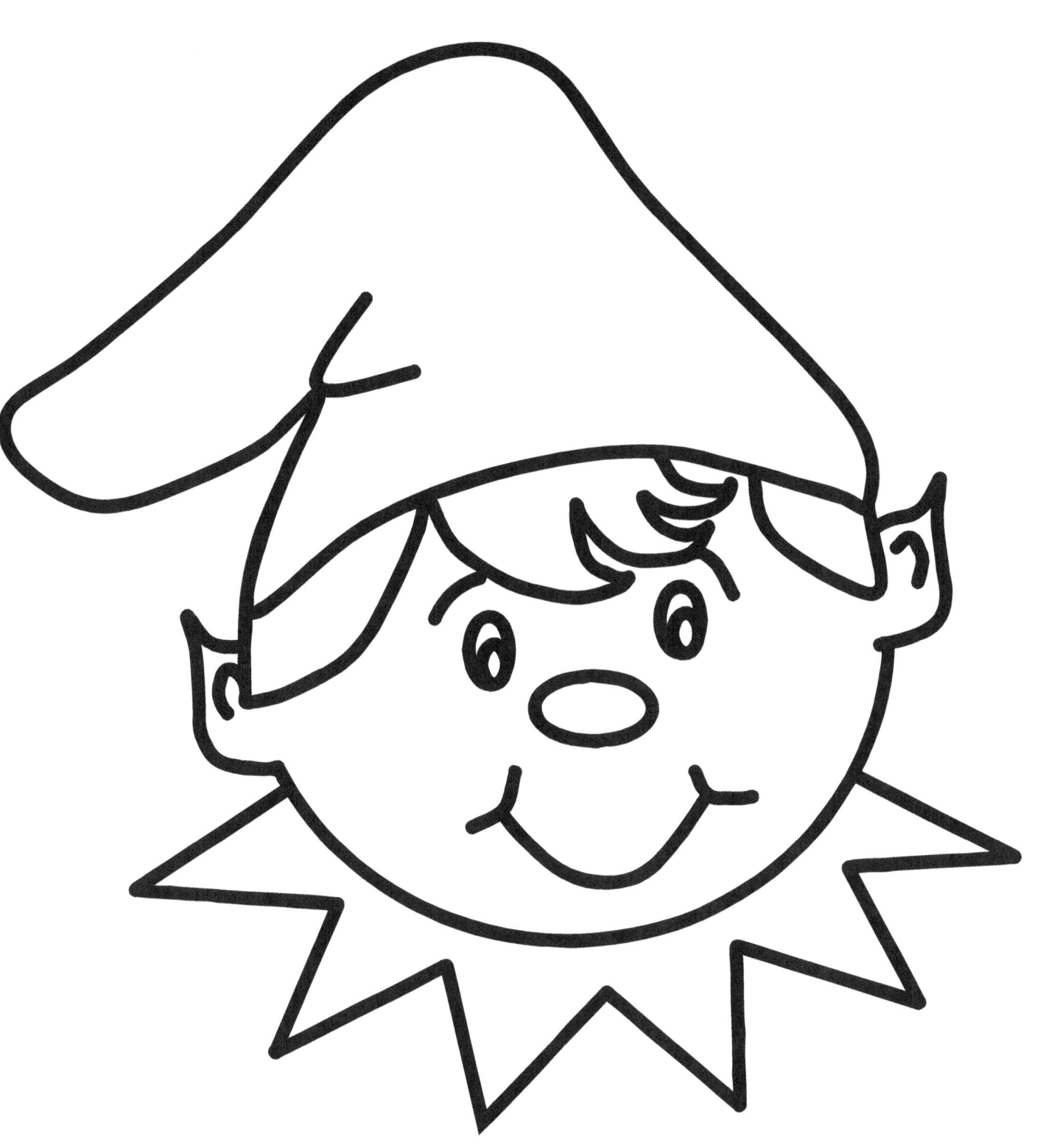

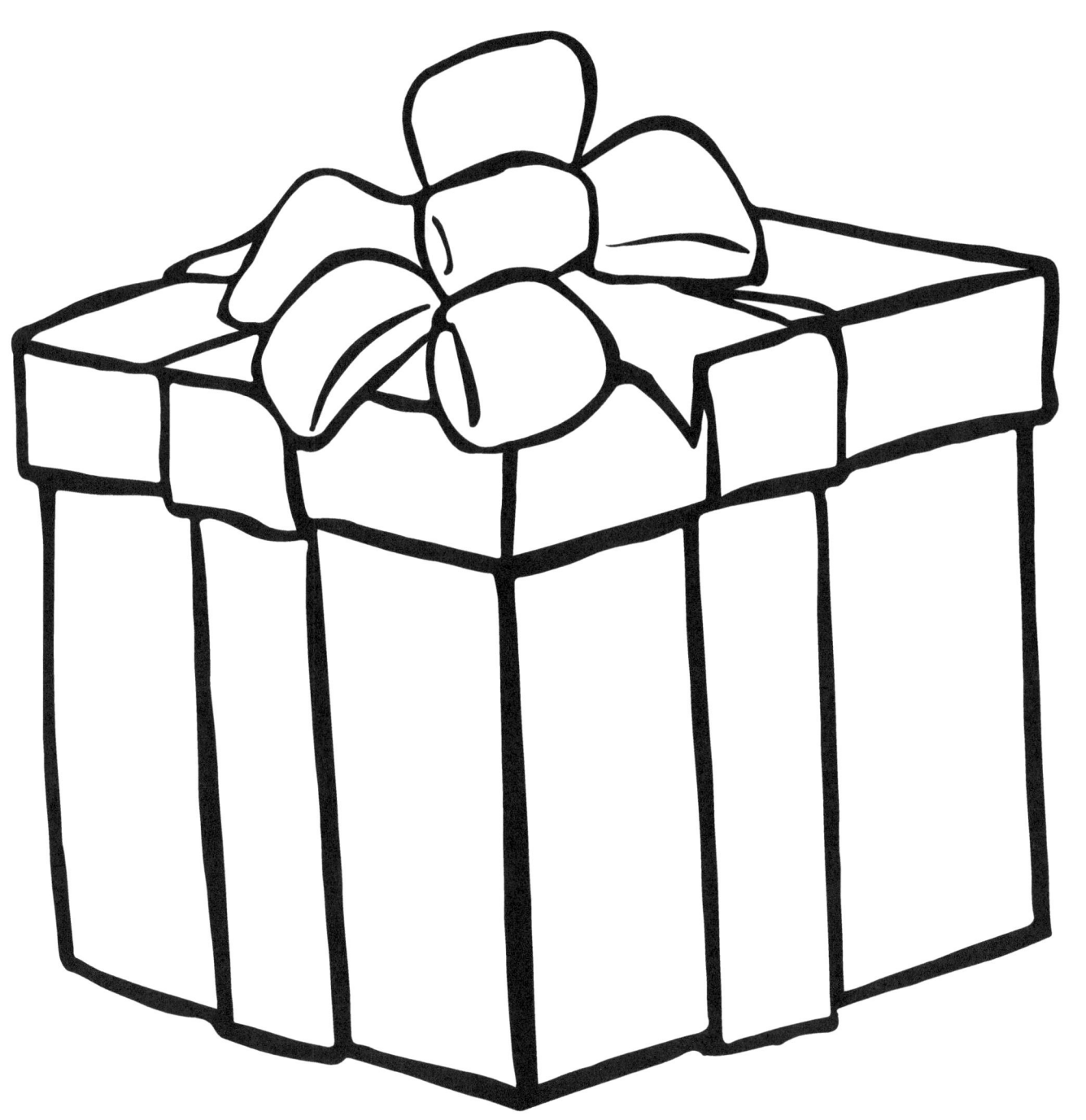

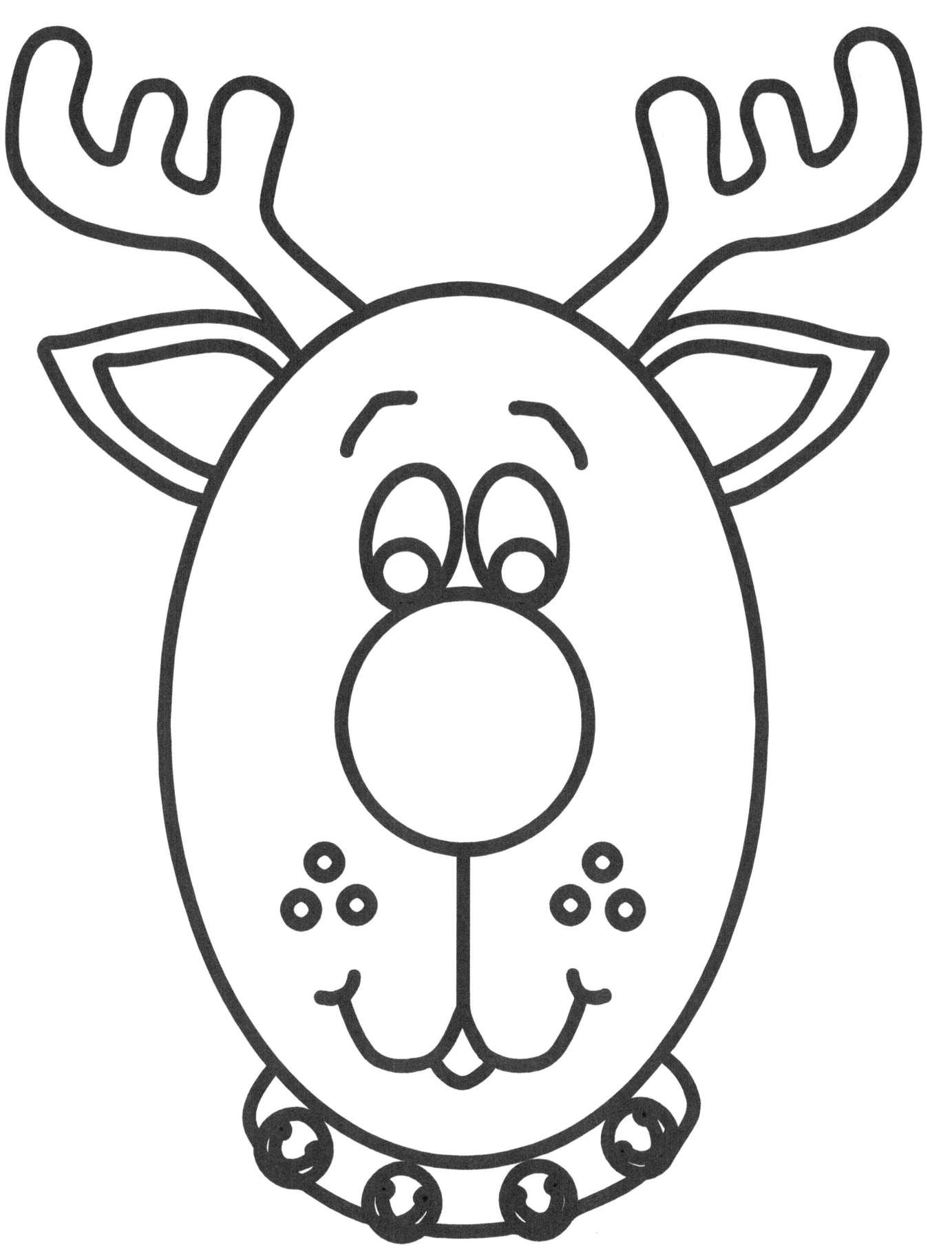

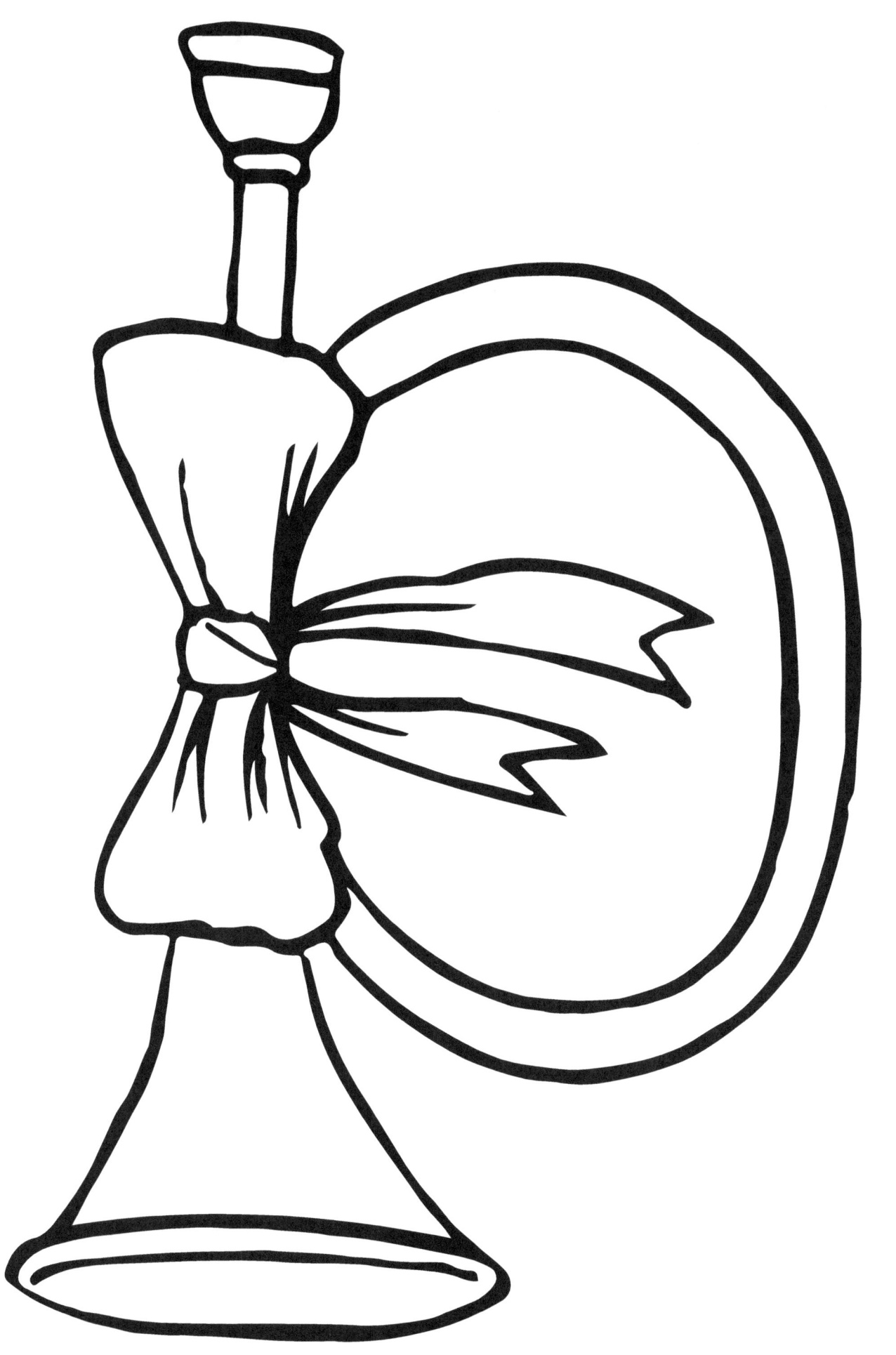

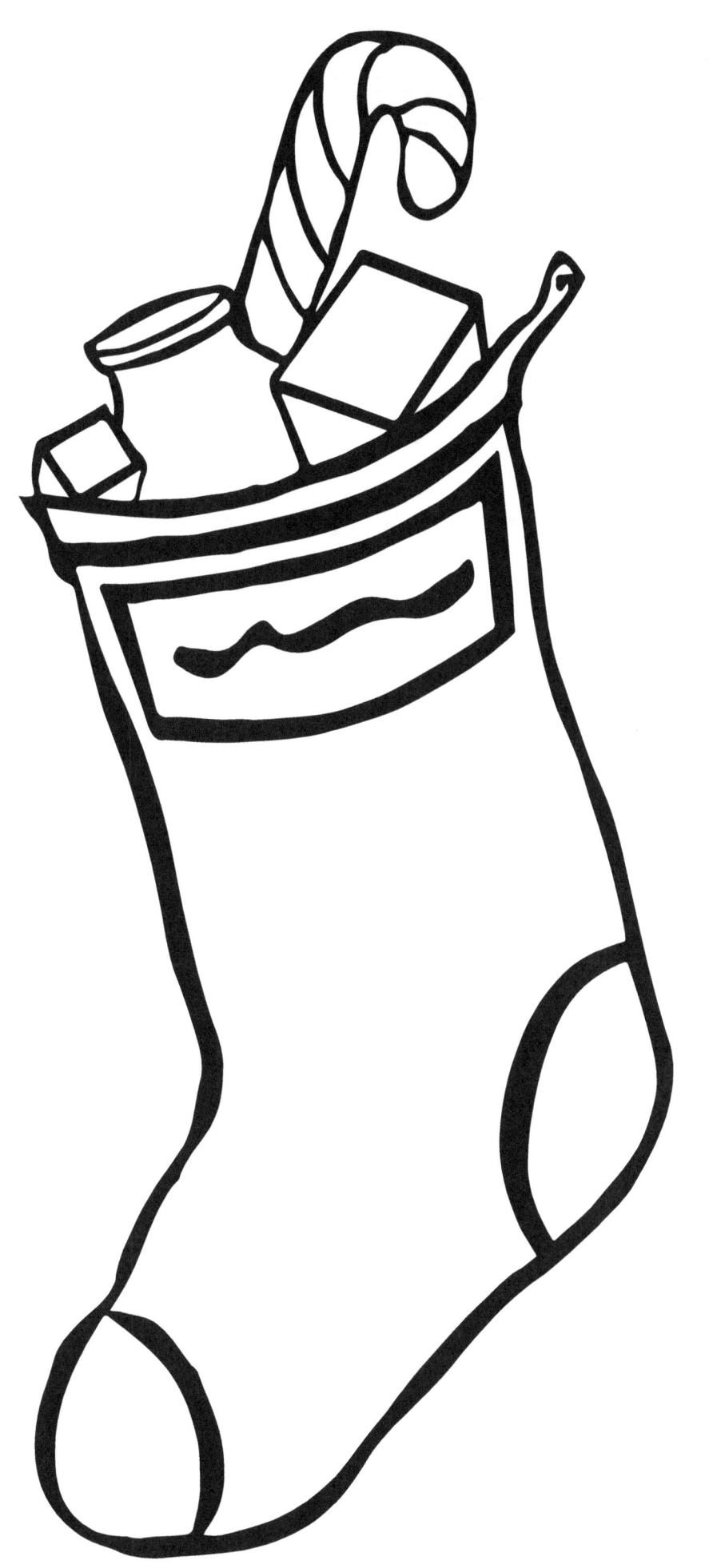

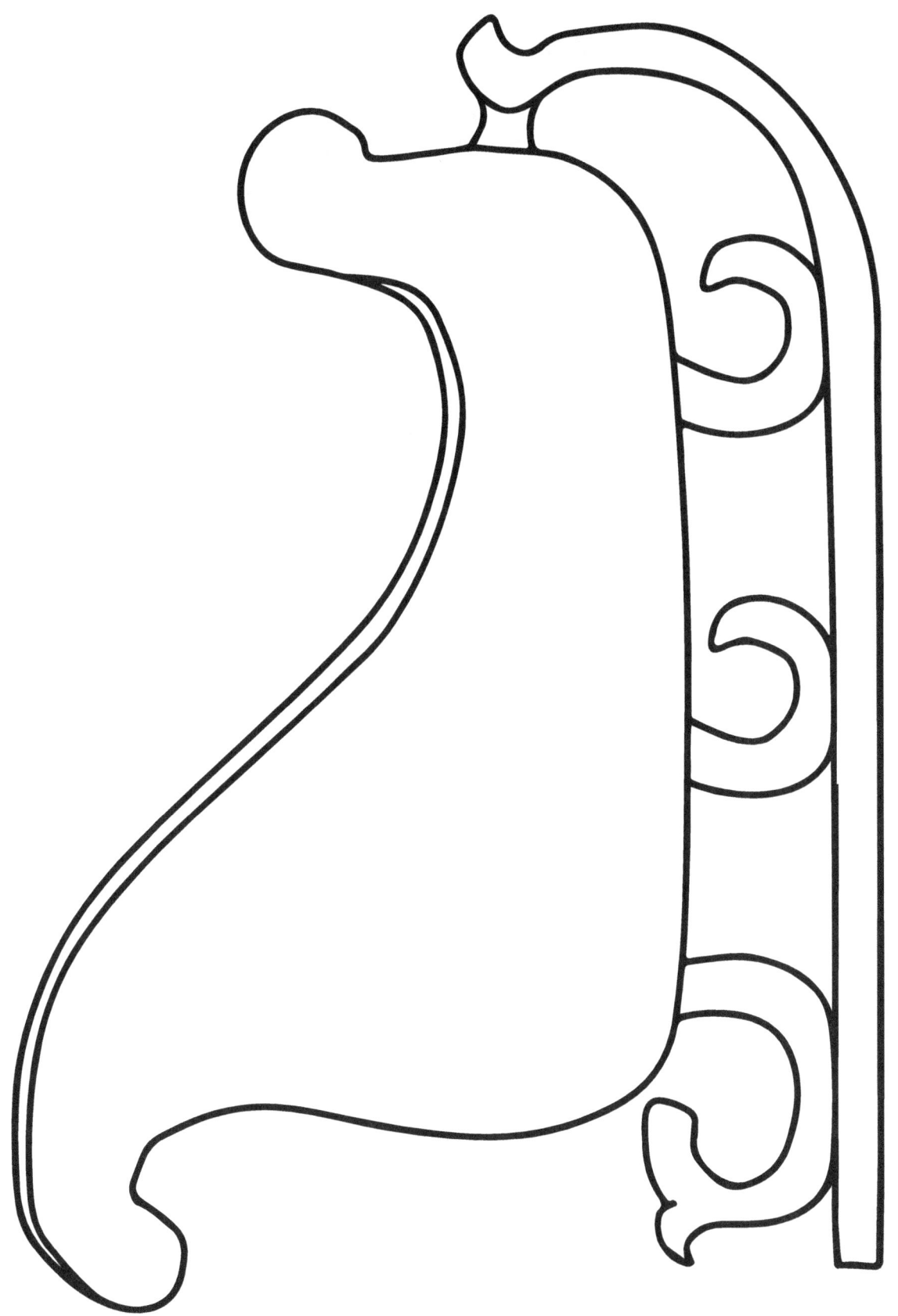

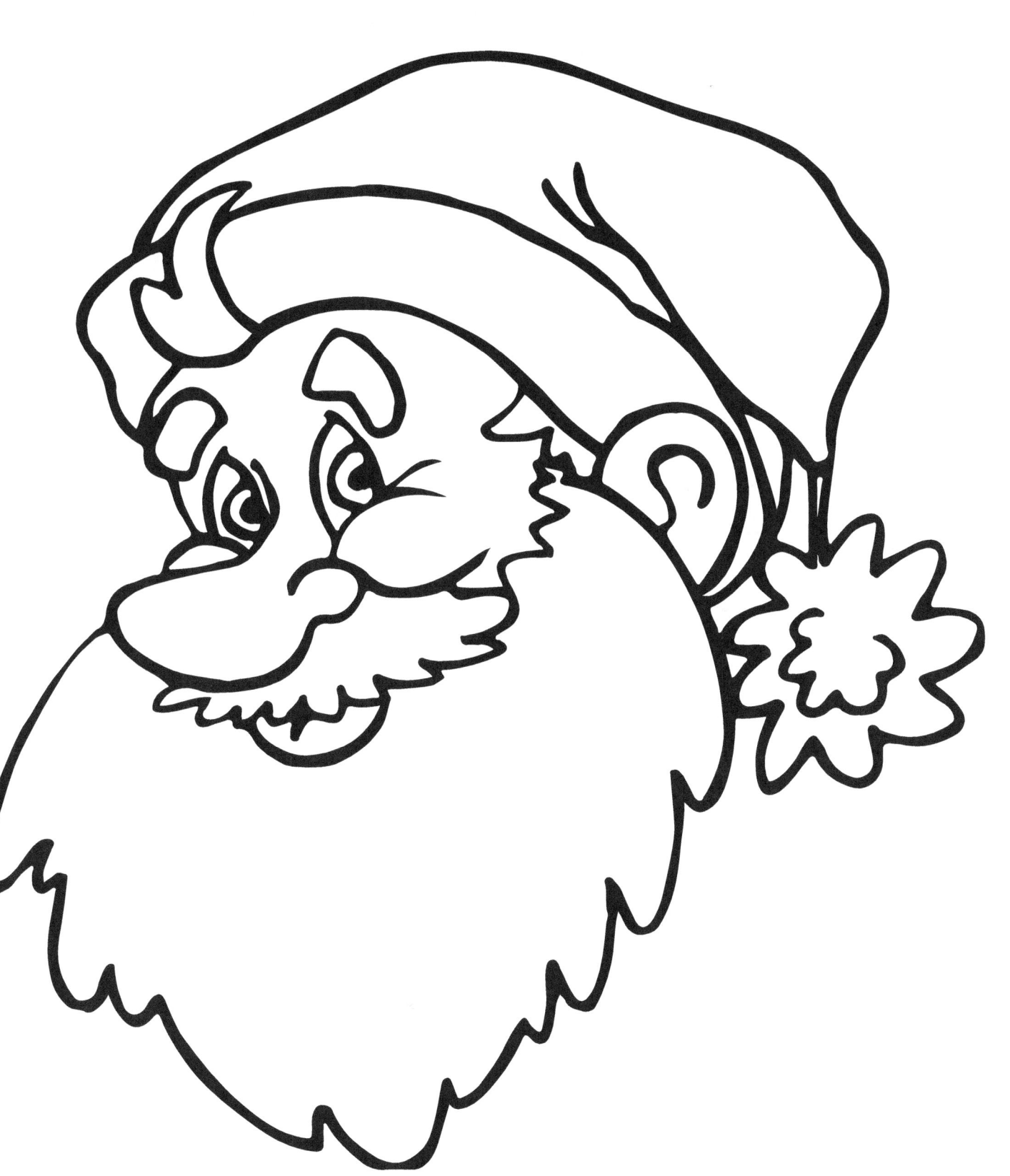

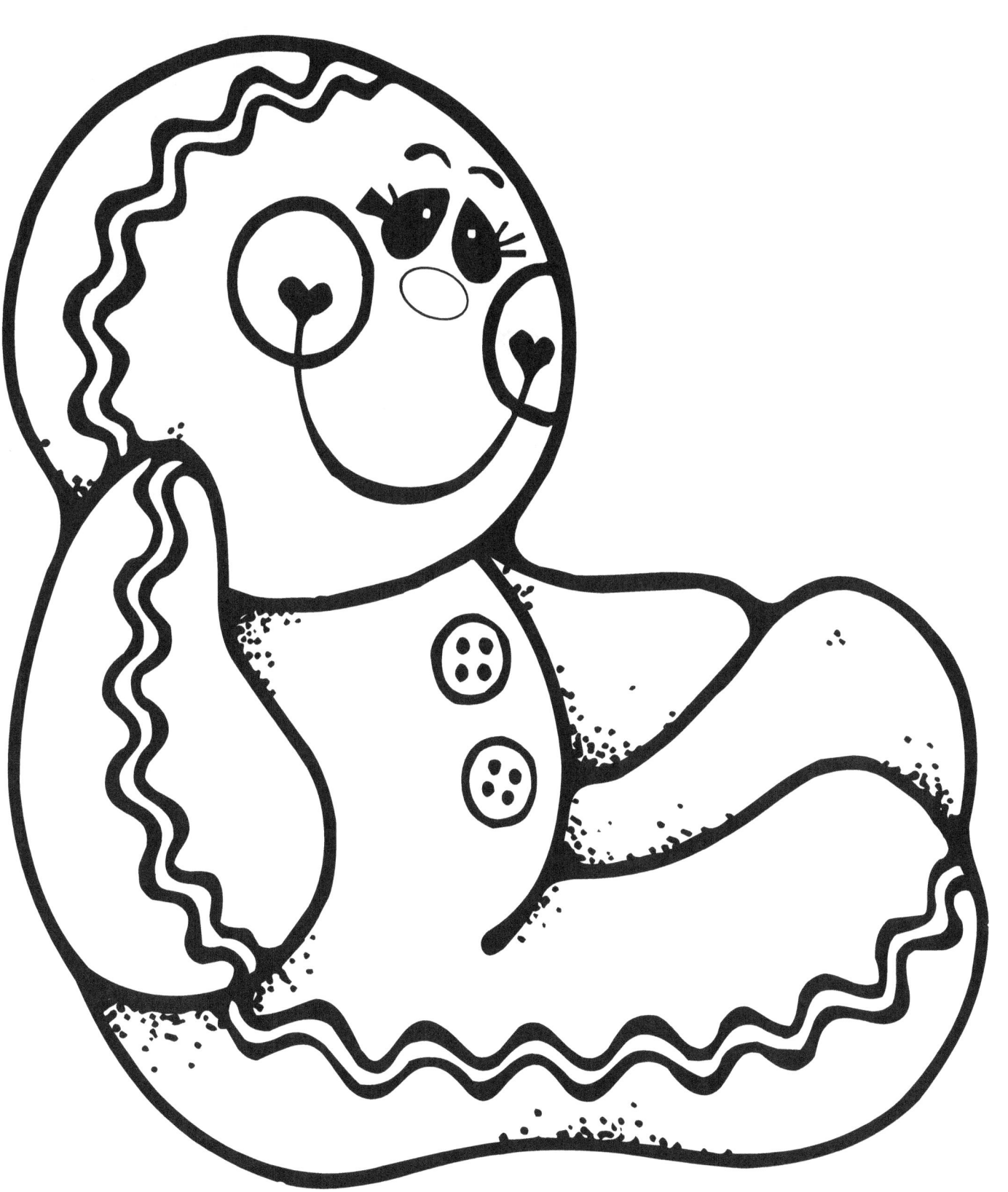

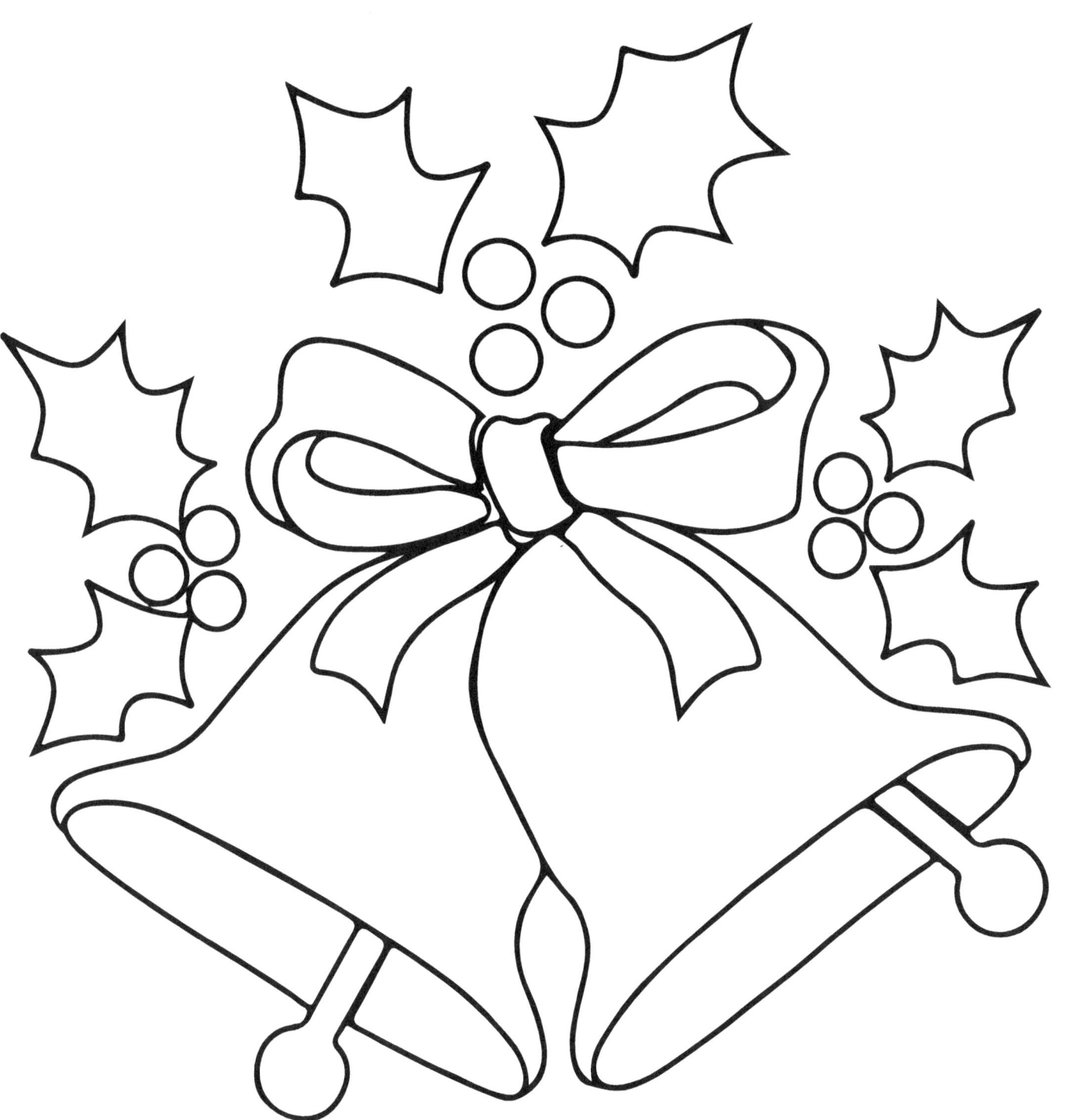

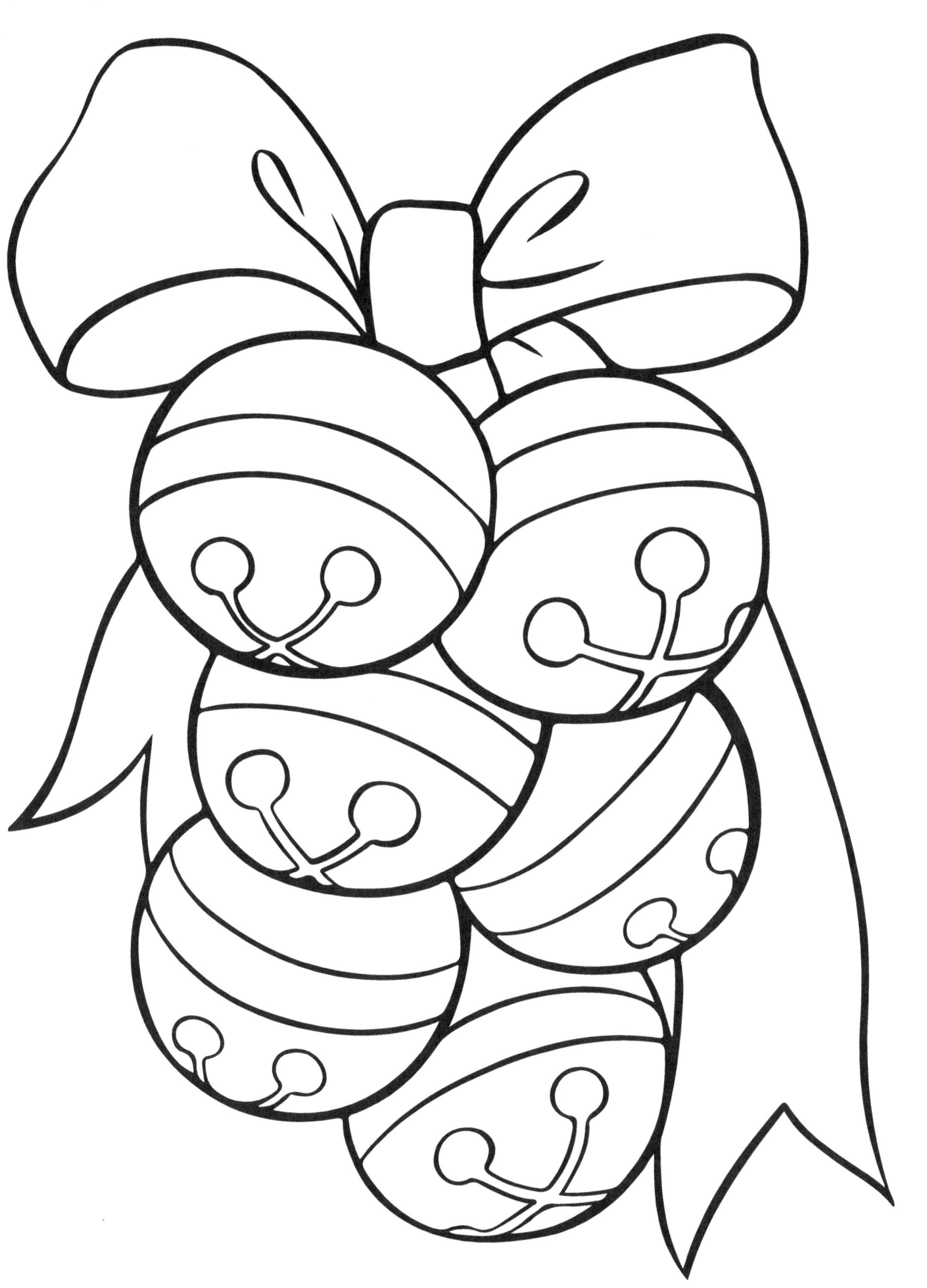

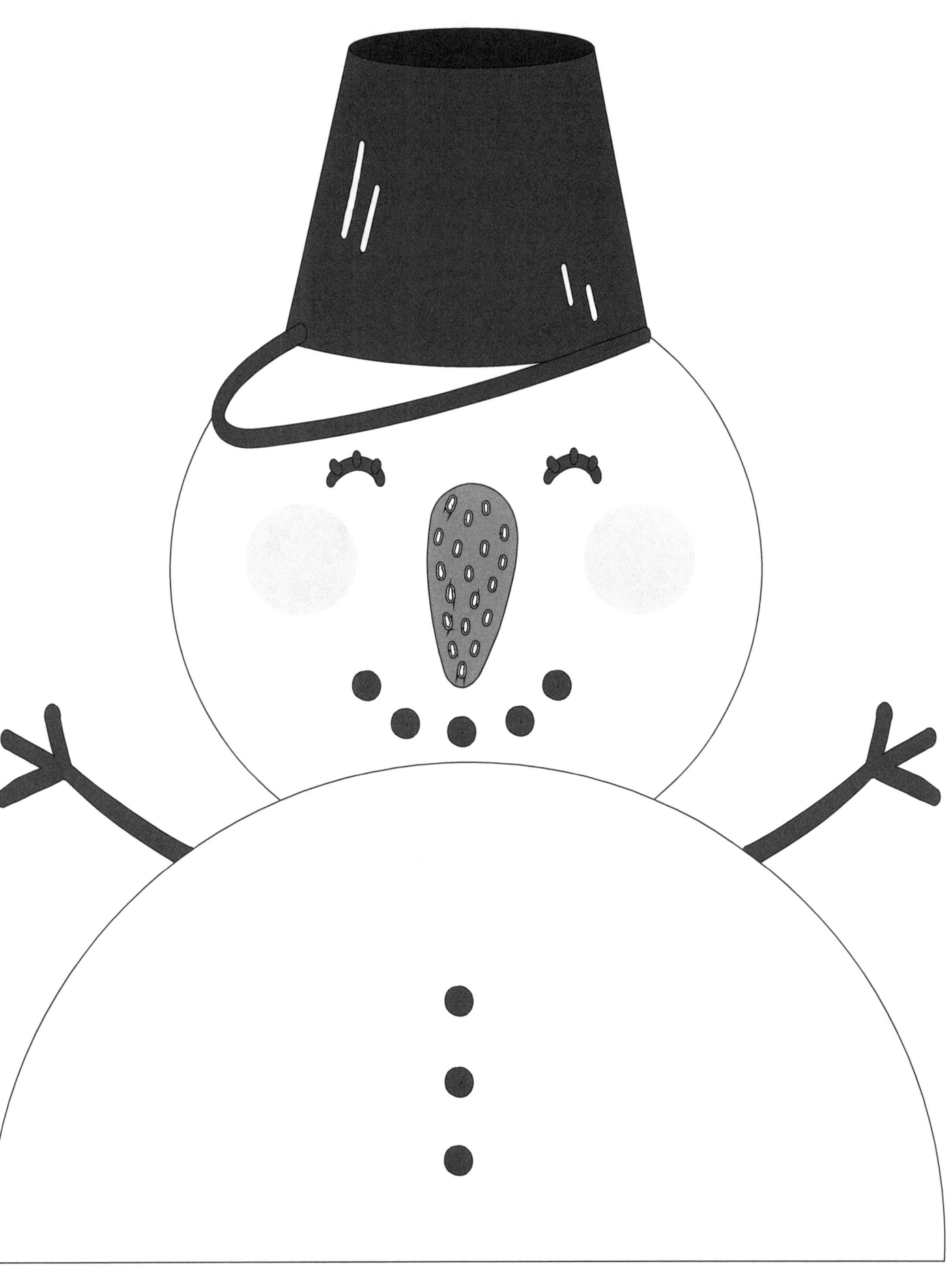

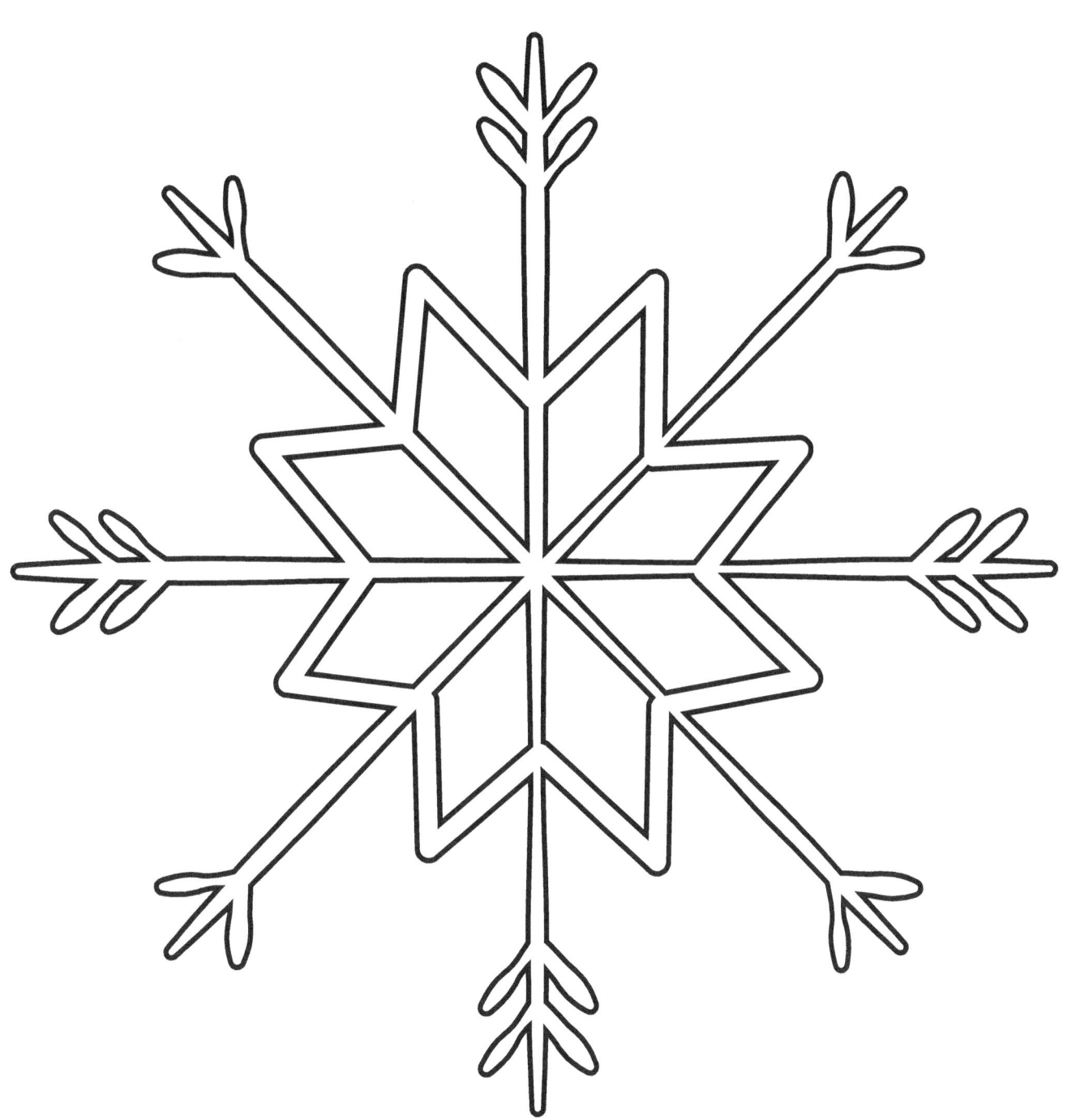

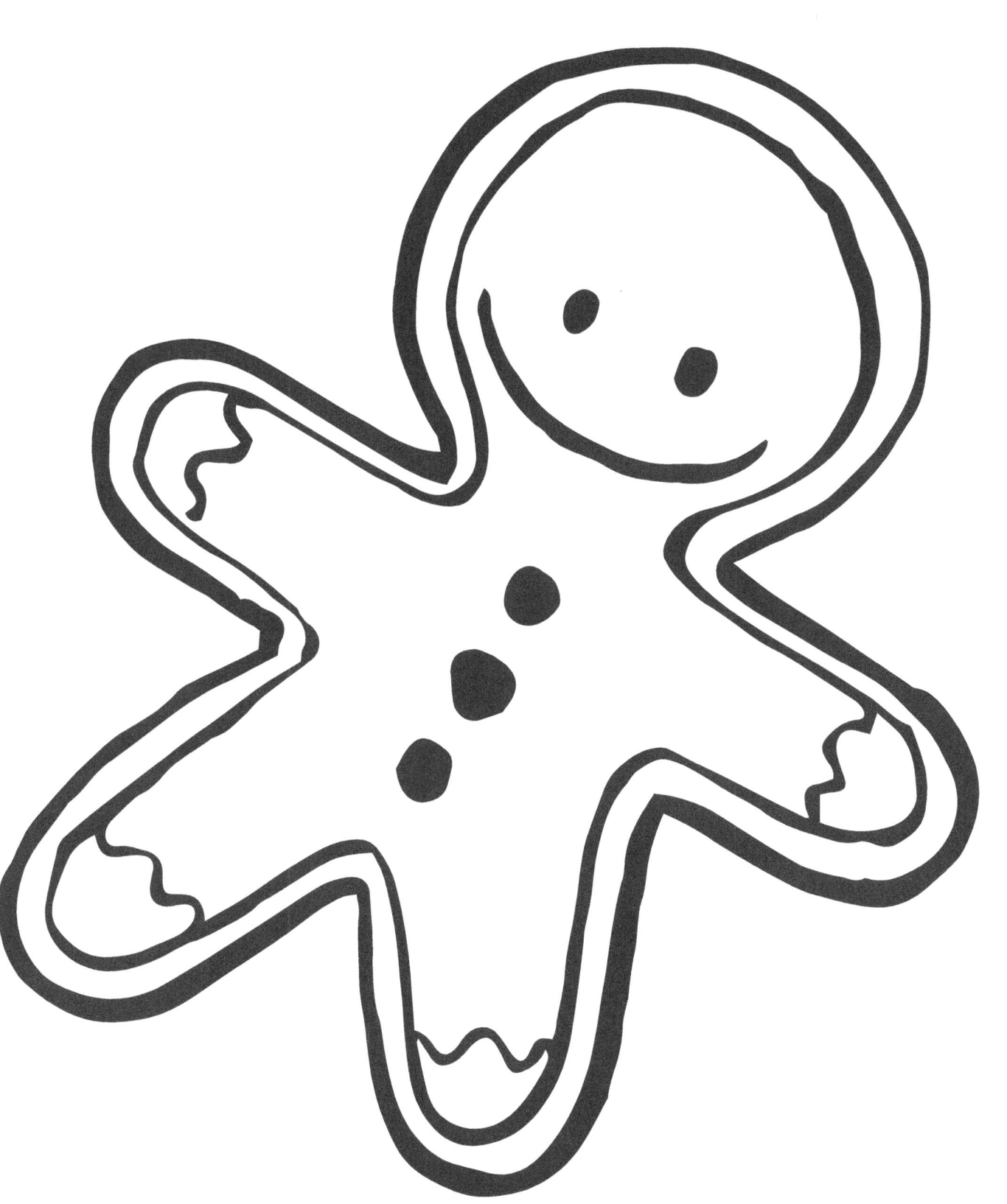

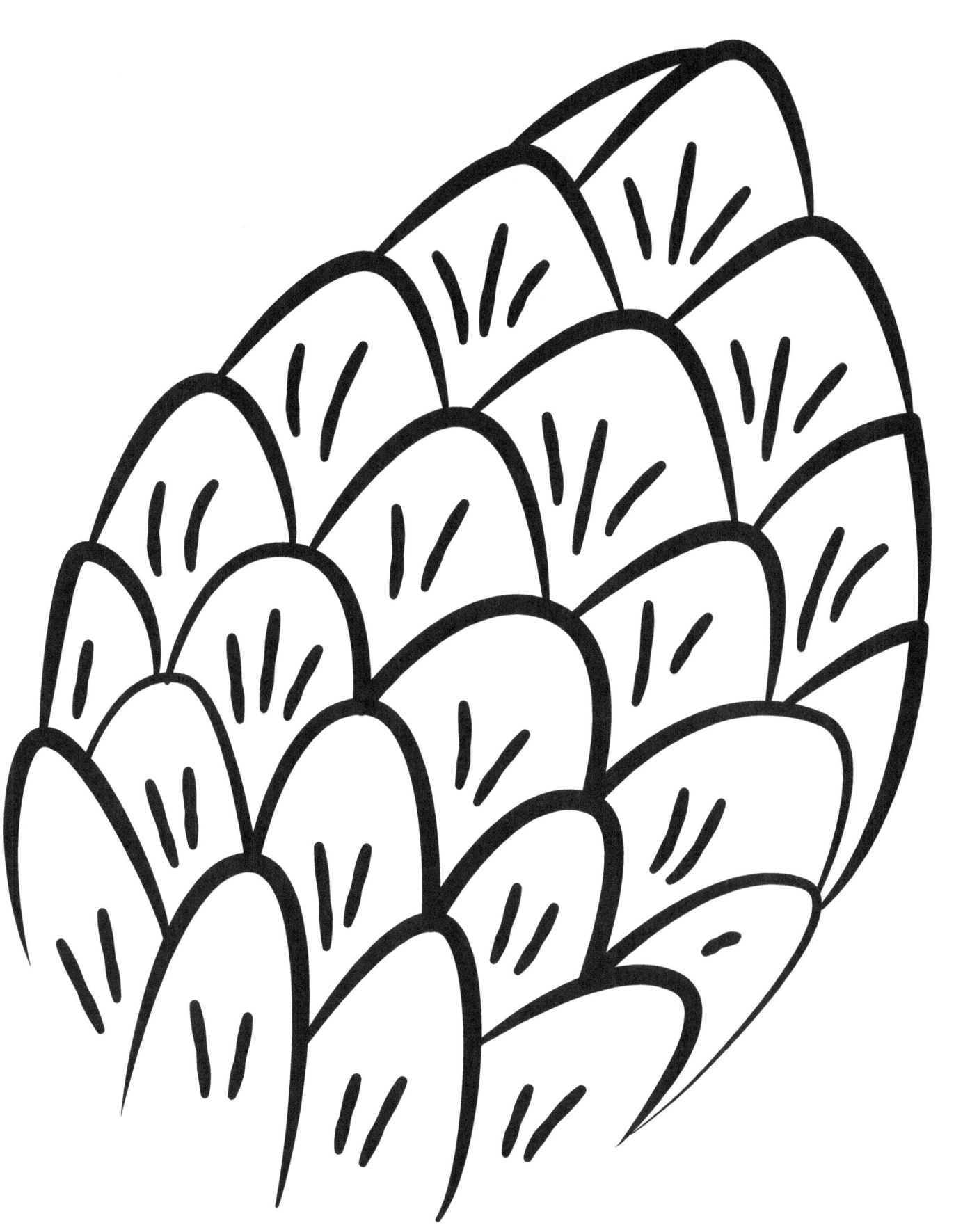

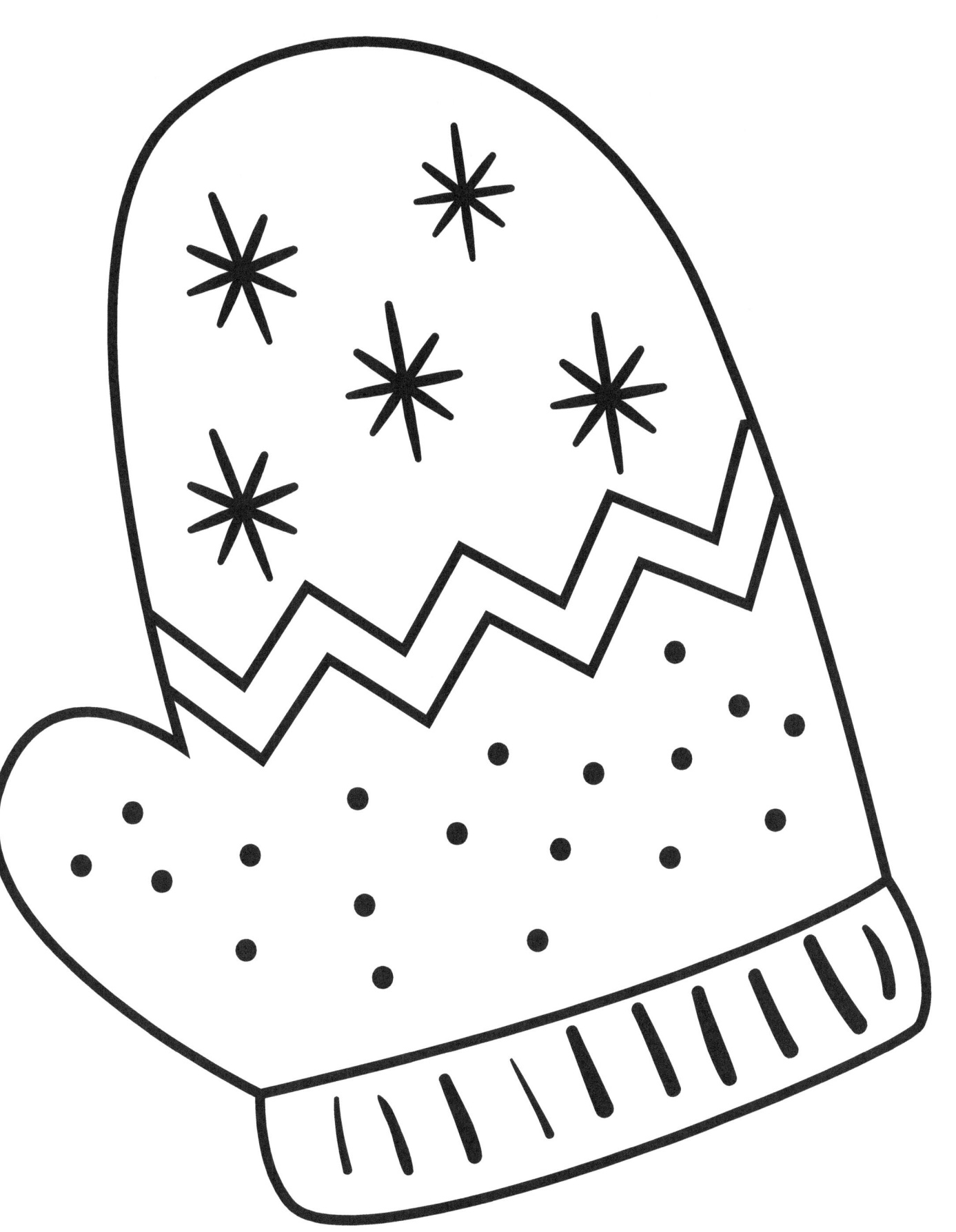

Merry Christmas

Merry Christmas & Happy New Year!

www.ingramcontent.com/pod-product-compliance
Lightning Source LLC
Chambersburg PA
CBHW081619220526
45468CB00010B/2947